SEVEN WONDERS OF THE NATURAL WORLD

A MyReportLinks.com Book

Amy Graham

MyReportLinks.com Books

an imprint of

 Enslow Publishers, Inc.

Box 398, 40 Industrial Road
Berkeley Heights, NJ 07922
USA

MyReportLinks.com Books, an imprint of Enslow Publishers, Inc. MyReportLinks®
is a registered trademark of Enslow Publishers, Inc.

Copyright © 2005 by Enslow Publishers, Inc.

Library of Congress Cataloging-in-Publication Data

Graham, Amy.
  Seven wonders of the natural world / Amy Graham.
    p. cm. — (Seven wonders of the world)
  Includes bibliographical references and index.
  ISBN 0-7660-5290-7
  1. Landforms—Juvenile literature. 2. Natural monuments—Juvenile literature.
I. Title. II. Series.
  GB406.G73 2005
  910'.02—dc22
                                        2004009085

Printed in the United States of America

10 9 8 7 6 5 4 3 2 1

To Our Readers:
Through the purchase of this book, you and your library gain access to the Report Links that specifically back
up this book.
The Publisher will provide access to the Report Links that back up this book and will keep these Report Links
up to date on **www.myreportlinks.com** for five years from the book's first publication date.
We have done our best to make sure all Internet addresses in this book were active and appropriate when we went
to press. However, the author and the Publisher have no control over, and assume no liability for, the material
available on those Internet sites or on other Web sites they may link to.
The usage of the MyReportLinks.com Books Web site is subject to the terms and conditions stated on the Usage
Policy Statement on **www.myreportlinks.com**.
A password may be required to access the Report Links that back up this book. The password is found on the
bottom of page 4 of this book.
Any comments or suggestions can be sent by e-mail to comments@myreportlinks.com or to the address on the
back cover.

Photo Credits: © 1995–2004 Public Broadcasting Service (PBS), p. 12; © 1996–2004 National Geographic
Society, pp. 13, 23; © 1997 Cable News Network, Inc., p. 6; © 1999–2001 Regents of the University of
California, p. 33; © 2002–2004 The Everest Peace Project, p. 11; © 2003 by MWW, p. 7; © 2003
Nordlyssenteret, p. 31; © 2004 The University of South Dakota, p. 22; © Corel Corporation, pp. 3, 8, 9, 15,
19, 24, 28, 29, 38, 41; © Sigurdur H Stefnisson, p. 32; © Zambia National Tourist Board, p. 17; Department
of the Environment and Heritage (Aus.), p. 26; Earth Observatory/National Aeronautics and Space
Administration, p. 27; Ibis Communications, Inc., p. 16; MyReportLinks.com Books, p. 4; National Archives,
pp. 34, 36; Photos.com, p. 1; University of North Dakota, p. 37; U.S. Department of the Interior, p. 20;
Wonderclub.com, p. 40.

Cover Photo: Photos.com

Cover Description: The Grand Canyon in Arizona, United States of America.

CONTENTS

MyReportLinks.com Books
Great Books, Great Links, Great for Research!

The Internet sites featured in this book can save you hours of research time. These Internet sites—we call them **"Report Links"**—are constantly changing, but we keep them up to date on our Web site.

When you see this "Approved Web Site" logo, you will know that we are directing you to a great Internet site that will help you with your research.

Give it a try! Type http://www.myreportlinks.com into your browser, click on the series title and enter the password, then click on the book title, and scroll down to the Report Links listed for this book.

The Report Links will bring you to great source documents, photographs, and illustrations. MyReportLinks.com Books save you time, feature Report Links that are kept up to date, and make report writing easier than ever! A complete listing of the Report Links can be found on pages 42–43 at the back of the book.

Please see "To Our Readers" on the copyright page for important information about this book, the MyReportLinks.com Web site, and the Report Links that back up this book.

Please enter **SWN1882** if asked for a password.

Seven Wonders of the Natural World Facts

Mount Everest, Nepal/Tibet

* Tallest mountain on earth at an elevation of 29,035 feet (8,850 meters)
* First ascended on May 29, 1953, by New Zealander Sir Edmund Hillary and Sherpa Tenzing Norgay
* First person to ascend alone without supplemental oxygen was Reinhold Messner from Italy in 1980
* First woman to ascend Everest was Junko Tabei from Japan in 1975

Victoria Falls, Zambia/Zimbabwe

* The mile-wide Zambezi River drops 355 feet (108 meters) into a narrow gorge
* Spray from the falls forms a mist visible for miles

Grand Canyon, Arizona

* A one-mile-deep chasm in the earth
* Nearly 300 miles (483 kilometers) long and 18 miles (29 kilometers) wide
* Over 4 million visitors a year
* Exposed rock is up to 1.8 billion years old

Great Barrier Reef, Australia

* A limestone reef built by sea animals called corals
* Stretches 1,250 miles (2,012 kilometers) along the northeast coast of Australia
* One of the most bio-diverse habitats on the planet

Northern Lights

* Glowing, flickering lights in the night sky near the North Pole
* Made by solar winds interacting with the earth's atmosphere
* Occurs 60 miles (97 kilometers) above the earth's surface

Paricutín Volcano, Mexico

* A young volcano that grew out of a farmer's cornfield
* Grew to 1,391 feet (424 meters) over nine-year life span
* Destroyed two villages

Harbor of Rio de Janeiro, Brazil

* A beautiful, tropical harbor with a one-mile (1.6-kilometer) wide entrance
* Famous for its sandy beaches of Ipanema and Copacabana
* Rio de Janeiro is the second-largest city in Brazil

NATURE'S WONDERS

The ancient Greeks and Romans first came up with the idea. They listed the most incredible sights of their time and called them the Seven Wonders of the World. The wonders of the Roman world included statues, a temple, pyramids, and a lighthouse. All were man-made. In those days people, not machines,

Destination: The Natural Wonders of the World - Microsoft Internet Explorer

File   Edit   View   Favorites   Tools   Help

Address http://www.cnn.com/TRAVEL/DESTINATIONS/9711/natural.wonders/   Go   Links »

TRAVEL NEWS
DESTINATIONS
CITY GUIDES
GETTING READY
CURRENCY

SEARCH
FEEDBACK

THE SEVEN
NATURAL WONDERS
OF THE WORLD

"We can never have enough of nature. We must be refreshed by the sight of inexhaustible vigor, vast and titanic features, the sea-coast with its wrecks, the wilderness with its living and its decaying trees, the thunder-cloud, and the rain which lasts three weeks and produces freshets. We need to witness our own limits transgressed, and some life pasturing freely where we never wander."

--- Henry David Thoreau

GRAND CANYON   NORTHERN LIGHTS   MT. EVEREST

PARICUTIN

THE HARBOR AT RIO DE JANEIRO   VICTORIA FALLS   THE GREAT BARRIER REEF

APPROVED WEB SITE

Done

Although there is no definitive list of the Seven Wonders of the Natural World, many agree that they consist of the Northern Lights, the Grand Canyon, Paricutín volcano, the harbor at Rio de Janeiro, Victoria Falls, Mount Everest, and the Great Barrier Reef. Learn more about these at this CNN Web page called **The Seven Natural Wonders of the World**.

EDITOR'S CHOICE

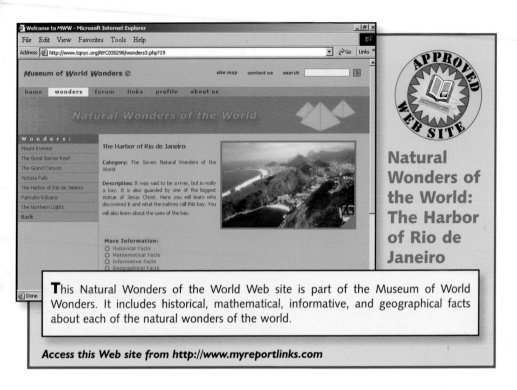

This Natural Wonders of the World Web site is part of the Museum of World Wonders. It includes historical, mathematical, informative, and geographical facts about each of the natural wonders of the world.

Access this Web site from http://www.myreportlinks.com

did the hard labor. Buildings were amazing feats of human power. Most ancient wonders exist today only in stories. Only the Great Pyramid of Egypt, built around 2550 B.C., still stands.

The tradition of listing the Seven Wonders of the World carries on. Unlike the "Wonders of the Ancient World," people can claim none of the glory for creating the "Wonders of the Natural World." Nature alone carved these sights that we so admire. Over the course of millions of years, rivers flowed over their rocky beds. Slowly the water eroded the stone, carving waterfalls and canyons. Volcanoes and mountains thrust up from the earth in reaction to movement far beneath the ground. Powerful forces of nature shaped the land we know today.

The natural world is a beautiful place. From the ocean shores to the inland forests, there are many little spots of heaven on earth. It is not easy choosing the top seven wonders. Not every person agrees on each selection. Still, some places are unquestionably a

▲ *The mysterious, flickering Northern Lights.*

touch above all the rest. The world's tallest mountain, a beautiful harbor, a terrifying volcano, a waterfall, a canyon, a coral reef, and a phenomenon in the night sky—these are the Seven Wonders of the Natural World. They are the most magnificent views nature has to offer.

What do these seven eye-catching things have in common? From the thundering Victoria Falls to the mysterious, flickering Northern Lights, the wonders leave humans awestruck. They are so spectacular that people have a hard time comprehending what they are seeing. In times of old, people told myths and legends to explain what they could not understand. By the twenty-first century A.D., scientists had explained away much of the mystery of these wonders. Yet they remain astonishing sights of nature. They are awesome examples of what the forces of nature can accomplish over the course of millions of years.

Chapter 2

MOUNT EVEREST

The lofty and striking Himalayan Mountains is one of the world's youngest mountain ranges. Their jagged peaks tower above and along the border of Nepal and Tibet, China. The crown jewel of the Himalayas, Mount Everest, stands above them all. Its peak is the highest point on earth. *Himalayas* is a Sanskrit word that means "home of the snow." Sanskrit is an ancient language that originated in the area that is modern-day India. The Khumbu glacier covers Everest in a blanket of white all year long.

▲ A view of Mount Everest from Kala Patar. Many climbers use Kala Patar as a launch point to begin their trek up Everest.

Rumbling avalanches and the howling wind are the only noises that disrupt the quiet.

Birth of the Himalayas

Geologists are scientists that study the rocks that form our planet. Geologists discovered the earth's crust is broken into about a dozen large pieces called plates. These huge plates constantly shift and move in reaction to changes deep within the earth. Sometimes plates grind into each other, and sometimes they move apart, creating a rift. Plates can also rub against each other as they move. This process of crust movement is called plate tectonics. Tectonic plates are the building blocks of the earth's crust. Both continents and ocean floors sit on top of tectonic plates. Sixty million years ago, India, then a separate continent, crashed into Asia. The collision caused the land to thrust up and form a new mountain range, the Himalayas.

In the mid-1800s, a British survey of India called the Great Trigonometrical Survey of India, mapped the Himalayas. The surveyors discovered a tall mountain they called Peak XV, now known as Mount Everest. They calculated Peak XV had an elevation of 29,002 feet (8,840 meters). They had found the highest mountain on the planet. Estimates of the mountain's elevation varied over the years. It was settled in 1998 when an American placed a Global Positioning System (GPS) device on Everest's peak. GPS technology uses satellites to map the earth's surface. The exact elevation of Mount Everest is now known to be 29,035 feet (8,850 meters), and it continues to grow. Every year the mountain gains a quarter of an inch in height. The colliding tectonic plates, always in motion, continue to drive the Himalayas skyward.[1]

The Ultimate Challenge

The British named their find after Sir George Everest, a supervisor of the Survey of India. The Tibetans call it *Chha-mo-lung-ma*, meaning "district of the birds." In Nepal, it is called *Sagarmatha*,

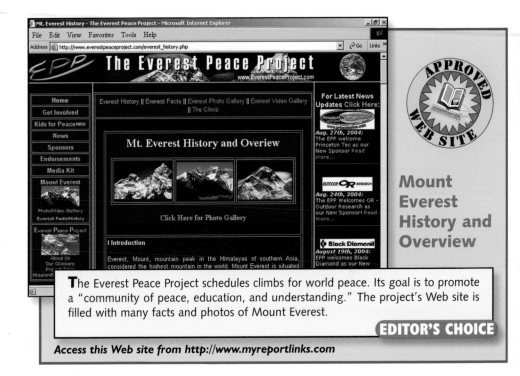

The Everest Peace Project schedules climbs for world peace. Its goal is to promote a "community of peace, education, and understanding." The project's Web site is filled with many facts and photos of Mount Everest.

EDITOR'S CHOICE

Access this Web site from http://www.myreportlinks.com

or "sky head." From the time the Western world discovered Everest, mountain climbers longed to conquer the summit. They wished to experience the thrill of standing on top of the world. Also, if people could climb the world's highest peak, it would prove we could handle anything. But it was not so easily done. Mount Everest is in a very remote spot and is difficult to reach. Climbers needed permission to climb from the local governments. Both Tibet and Nepal were wary of Westerners. Nepal, for example, had fought a war against Great Britain from 1814 to 1816. Finally, in 1921, the Dalai Lama, the leader of Tibet, agreed to allow in a team of British climbers.

Access to the mountain region was only a small part of the challenge. Now the climbers had to transport tons of gear and supplies. The mountaineers found the help they needed in the Sherpa people of the Khumbu Valley. Originally from Tibet, Sherpas moved to the high mountain regions of Nepal in the

1500s. The expeditions hired Sherpas as guides and porters. The Sherpas quickly became known for their skill at climbing in high altitudes. The Sherpas' Buddhist religion teaches that the mountains are homes of the gods. Before climbing, Sherpas offer rice and incense to gain the mountain's blessing.[2]

On May 29, 1953, New Zealander Edmund Hillary and Sherpa Tenzing Norgay became the first to reach the top. Their success encouraged other climbers. Since 1953, over 1,200 people have stood on top of the world. New records for getting to the top the quickest are set each year. In 1963, the first Americans reached the summit. The first woman to climb Everest was Junko Tabei from Japan in 1975. In 2001, American Erik Weihenmayer became the first blind person on Everest.

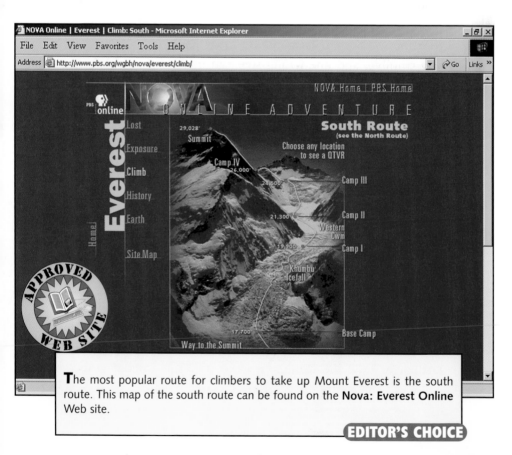

The most popular route for climbers to take up Mount Everest is the south route. This map of the south route can be found on the **Nova: Everest Online** Web site.

EDITOR'S CHOICE

One of the most amazing records is the one set by Reinhold Messner and Peter Habeler in 1978. They made it to the top without supplemental or additional oxygen. When the altitude is above 26,000 feet (7,925 meters) the air is very

Everest 50

Access this Web site from http://www.myreportlinks.com

Photos, maps, games, adventurous stories, and many other interactive features make this site a great way to learn about Mount Everest. See how well you do on the virtual climb of the world's tallest mountain!

thin. It contains only one third of the oxygen people need to breathe. Without enough oxygen, the human body begins to break down. People experience blindness and hallucinations. Their hearts race and their lungs strain to pull in more air. They may stumble, and one wrong step can mean certain death on a windy, icy slope. Sooner or later the brain shuts down. People can fall into a coma or even die.[3] Most climbers choose to carry the extra weight of oxygen tanks.

After eighty years of western sightseers, the Khumbu region was a different place. The base camps were strewn with trash. People had over-harvested forests for firewood. This has caused the government of Nepal to become more conservation minded. The country created Sagarmatha National Park in 1976. Today there are tree-planting programs to help the forests, and tourists are strongly encouraged to carry out their trash.[4] Everest continues to draw people to its slopes. New mountaineers come every year, hoping to set their own personal records.

VICTORIA FALLS

The Zambezi River flows lazily through southern-central Africa. The wide river begins in northern Zambia. From there it flows serenely south through Angola. As it reaches Botswana, the river swerves sharply east toward the sea. It forms the border between the two countries of Zambia and Zimbabwe. It is here the mile-wide river suddenly takes a plunge. Dropping abruptly over a 355-foot (108-meter) cliff, the river forms a waterfall of amazing proportions. The cascading water crashes into a narrow ravine, then takes a sharp turn into the Batoka Gorge. This is Victoria Falls, the world's widest waterfall. It is twice the width and depth of Niagara Falls.

Above the falls, the Zambezi River is broad and slow moving. The gorge below is much narrower. The channeled water in the gorge is no longer placid and calm. The water churns in rushing rapids. The stormy river zigzags over the next 5 miles (8 kilometers). The water searches for the path that offers the least resistance. The thundering waterfall sends up a cloud of mist that is visible for miles around. The sun shining through the spray forms colorful rainbows. One African name for the falls is *Shongwe,* meaning "rainbow."

▷ Dr. Livingstone

Dr. David Livingstone (1813–71) was the first European to see the falls. He was a medical doctor and a Christian missionary. Born in Scotland, he became famous for his explorations of Africa. In the mid-1800s, Livingstone was a well-known name in Great Britain, second only to the Queen.[1] Livingstone hoped to

Victoria Falls is the widest waterfall in the world. As the sun shines through the water it creates an almost ever-present rainbow.

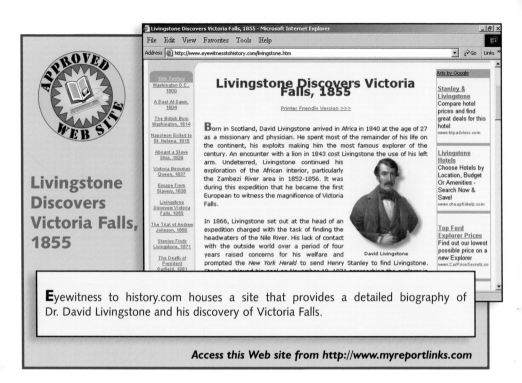

Livingstone Discovers Victoria Falls, 1855

Printer Friendly Version >>>

Born in Scotland, David Livingstone arrived in Africa in 1840 at the age of 27 as a missionary and physician. He spent most of the remainder of his life on the continent, his exploits making him the most famous explorer of the century. An encounter with a lion in 1843 cost Livingstone the use of his left arm. Undeterred, Livingstone continued his exploration of the African interior, particularly the Zambezi River area in 1852-1856. It was during this expedition that he became the first European to witness the magnificence of Victoria Falls.

In 1866, Livingstone set out at the head of an expedition charged with the task of finding the headwaters of the Nile River. His lack of contact with the outside world over a period of four years raised concerns for his welfare and prompted the *New York Herald* to send Henry Stanley to find Livingstone.

David Livingstone

Livingstone Discovers Victoria Falls, 1855

Eyewitness to history.com houses a site that provides a detailed biography of Dr. David Livingstone and his discovery of Victoria Falls.

Access this Web site from http://www.myreportlinks.com

bring his religion to the people of Africa. He was morally opposed to slavery. As he went about his travels, he worked to stop the slave trade. In 1855, Livingstone set out to explore the Zambezi River. He hoped to find a suitable shipping route to the Indian Ocean. Livingstone followed the Zambezi for about five hundred miles (eight hundred kilometers). Then the doctor met Sekeletu, chief of the Kololo people. Sekeletu brought Livingstone farther downstream to see the waterfall.[2] The Kololo people called the falls *Mosi-oa-Tunya*. This means "the smoke that thunders."

Of all the sights he saw during his travels, Livingstone thought the falls were the most amazing. He paddled a canoe to a large island on the edge of the falls. Later he remembered, "Creeping with awe to the verge, I peered down into a large [opening] which had been made from bank to bank of the broad Zambezi, and saw that a stream of a thousand yards broad leaped down a hundred feet and then became suddenly compressed into a space of fifteen to twenty yards."[3] Livingstone named the wondrous sight Victoria Falls after Queen Victoria.

Formation of the Falls

Victoria Falls is a cliff leading into a canyon. The falls cut into a layer of basalt rock that is 1,000 feet (300 meters) thick. Basalt is a volcanic rock formed from lava. As the lava cooled, cracks formed in the rock layer. Long ago, the Zambezi River began to flow over this zone of basalt rock. The rushing water found a fissure, or crack, in the rock. With the power of tons of flowing water, the river opened the fissure farther. The current swept the loose rock away. Over the course of many, many years, the

Victoria Falls has been described by a local tribe as "the Smoke that Thunders." Over 144.2 million gallons of water pass over the falls each minute when the Zambezi River is at its highest during flood season. **The Zambia National Tourist Board** Web site contains this image of Victoria Falls.

EDITOR'S CHOICE

waterfall was formed. Opposite the waterfall is another cliff. Spray from the falls keeps the cliff misty and damp. A lush rain forest grows there.

Not for the Fainthearted

Today there is a town called Livingstone near Victoria Falls. It is Zambia's number-one tourist destination. Also located there is Zambia's Mosi-oa-Tunya National Park, home to zebras, antelopes, giraffes, and a small population of endangered white rhinos.[4] On the Zimbabwe side is Victoria Falls National Park. People come from all over the world to view and catch the spray of the thundering water.

Recently, Victoria Falls has become a hot spot for extreme sports participants. Inspired by the spectacular falls, people try their own daring acts. Daredevils leap into the canyon from a bridge high above. A bungi rope secured to their ankles brings them back to safety. Brave souls can zoom across a zipline that reaches across Batoka Gorge.[5] Some say the best view of the falls is from above. Thrill seekers take in the view from a parachute. Others fly by the roaring river in a small plane called a microlight. Less daring tourists fly above the mist in helicopters. River sports like kayaking, canoeing, and white-water rafting are popular as well.

Chapter 4

THE GRAND CANYON

Walking up to the South Rim of the Grand Canyon, tourists have no warning of the majestic sight waiting just ahead. Suddenly the canyon comes into view. What a spectacular view it is. The earth drops away steeply to the canyon floor one mile (1.6 kilometers) below. Flat-topped buttes, striped with layers of rock, rise up from the canyon floor. The Colorado River snakes along the bottom of the gorge. At sunrise and sunset, the sun's rays light up the rock in shades of gold and crimson.

▲ This is a view of the Grand Canyon's North Rim in the state of Arizona. This is the highest part of the canyon.

The aptly named Grand Canyon is just that: a huge chasm in the earth. It stretches for 277 miles (446 kilometers) across northwestern Arizona. The canyon ranges from 4 to 18 miles (6 to 29 kilometers) wide. From the air, it looks like a big gash in the earth. From the ground, the immense scale is baffling to the human eye. Take, for example, the Spanish explorers who were the first Europeans to look down into the canyon in 1540. They thought that the Colorado River below was only about six feet (two meters) wide.[1] Their Hopi Indian guides explained the river was actually 300 to 400 feet (91 to 122 meters) across.

Three Distinct Climates

Most sightseers take in the view from the South Rim. The climate there is typical of the dry, southwestern United States. Forests of scraggly juniper, pinyon, and ponderosa pine stand along the canyon's edge. These trees withstand extreme temperatures and scarce rainfall. The canyon's North Rim, just 9 miles

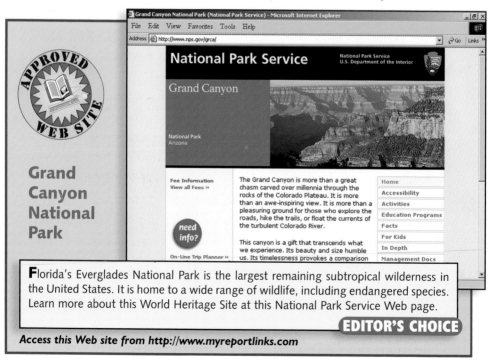

Grand Canyon National Park

Florida's Everglades National Park is the largest remaining subtropical wilderness in the United States. It is home to a wide range of wildlife, including endangered species. Learn more about this World Heritage Site at this National Park Service Web page.

EDITOR'S CHOICE

Access this Web site from http://www.myreportlinks.com

(14 kilometers) across the canyon from the South Rim, is 200 miles (322 kilometers) away by road. The elevation there is 1,000 feet (305 meters) higher than at the South Rim. Forests of pines, spruce, and aspen thrive in the North Rim's damp climate. Snowfall at these high altitudes makes roads impassable in the winter.

Down inside the canyon, the climate changes rapidly. Temperatures can spike to 118°F (48°C).[2] The canyon floor is home to desert plants like cacti, agave, and creosote bush. Rattlesnakes, bighorn sheep, and mountain lions live here. Hikers must carry plenty of water to survive a trip into the dry, hot canyon. A popular way to tour the area is by white-water raft. Paddlers take guided tours down the rapids of the Colorado River.

Reading the Rocks

The Grand Canyon contains some of the oldest exposed rock on earth. The rock, called Vishnu schist, was formed at least 1.7 billion years ago. These ancient rocks are almost half as old as our planet.[3] The Grand Canyon itself is much younger: only 5 million or 6 million years old. It was formed when two plates of the earth's crust collided. The land raised up, forming the Colorado Plateau. Then the Colorado River slowly carved through the plateau. Wind, rain, and snow also helped to erode the land. The river exposed layers of rock: sandstone, shale, limestone, granite, and schist. Geologists have discovered many fossils embedded in these rocks. Fossils show us what plants and animals lived when the rock was formed. There are fossils of ancient plants, reptiles, and insects. There are fish and other marine fossils. Hundreds of millions of years ago, this area lay at the bottom of an ocean.

People and the Grand Canyon

Compared to the ancient rock of the Grand Canyon, humans are newcomers to the area. American Indian tribes have lived here for the last four thousand years. The treasures of Grand Canyon National Park include over 2,700 preserved archaeological sites. There are the remains of old pueblos, cave and cliff dwellings where American Indians once lived.

For much of early American history, the Grand Canyon was a wild, unknown place. John Wesley Powell (1834–1902) brought the Grand Canyon into the public eye. Powell had a keen interest in geology and an adventurous spirit. A Civil War veteran, he had lost one arm in a battle. In 1869, the explorer led a team of nine men down the Colorado River. They took four bulky, wooden boats. Without maps of the area, the men had little idea what kind of perilous adventure lay in store. Only six of the group

Although its depth and width vary, in general, it takes a visitor on foot or by mule two days to travel from the top of the canyon to the bottom. Many good images, including this one, can be found at the **Grand Canyon Slides** Web page.

Grand Canyon National Park: National Geographic

Take a virtual tour of the Grand Canyon at this Web site. View photographs of the different parts of this natural wonder as you read about them. Enjoy traveling to the North and South rims, as well as notable areas nearby.

Access this Web site from http://www.myreportlinks.com

lived to tell the tale of their reckless trip. Powell was so captivated by the beauty of the canyon that he returned in 1871.

Preserved for the Future

President Theodore Roosevelt visited the Grand Canyon in 1903. He said, "Leave it as it is. You can not improve upon it. The ages have been at work on it and man can only mar it. What you can do is to keep it for your children, and your children's children, and for all who come after you, as one of the great sights which every American if he can travel at all should see."[4] In the last one hundred years, people have taken great interest in the Grand Canyon. Grand Canyon National Park was established in 1919. In 1975, the park expanded to its present size of 1,904 square miles (4,931 square kilometers). Once the Grand Canyon was an unmapped wilderness. Today more than 4 million tourists visit it each year.

GREAT BARRIER REEF

Looking down from space, astronauts can clearly see the Great Barrier Reef. It stretches for 1,250 miles (2,011 kilometers) along the tropical, northeast coast of Australia. Roughly the size of Japan, the reef is the largest structure on earth made by living beings. Tiny sea creatures called coral have built the reefs over the past 2 million years. The Great Barrier Reef, in spite of its name, is really 2,900 or more individual coral reefs. The reef attaches to

▲ *There is an abundance of marine life living along the Great Barrier Reef. This photo was taken off the coast of Queensland.*

the edge of Australia's continental shelf. It stands in shallow water that is 325 to 650 feet (99 to 198 meters) deep. On the side facing the Pacific Ocean, the seafloor sharply drops down thousands of feet.

Size alone would be enough to put the Great Barrier Reef on the list of top wonders of the world, but that is far from all. Up close the reefs have a magical quality. The water of the Coral Sea is a clear, bright blue. The reefs burst with color like a flower garden in full bloom. Pastel fans of soft coral gently sway in the tide. Brilliantly colored fish dart in and out of the protection of the reefs. The reefs keep the ocean waves at bay. Sea grass and mangrove trees grow in the calm lagoons between the reefs and the shore. Islands rise up from the ocean floor. Some were hills on land before the glaciers melted and the ocean rose around them. Other islands are cays, or coral reefs that have become islands.

The Great Barrier Reef is one of the most diverse ecosystems in the world. An amazing variety of animals and plants live here. It is home to more than 1,500 species of fish, 4,000 species of mollusks, and 30 species of whales and dolphins. Endangered humpback whales come here from the Antarctic to give birth. Threatened sea turtles breed here. There are sea worms, shrimp, sponges, starfish, sea urchins, squid, and sharks. New species are discovered here every month.[1]

▷ Builders of the Sea

A coral reef is made of a porous rock called limestone. Over four hundred different species of coral live in the Great Barrier Reef. Not all kinds of coral build reefs. The reef-building corals are hard, stony corals. They live together in groups called colonies. Each stony coral absorbs dissolved limestone from the ocean water. Using the limestone, the animal builds a skeleton for itself. When the coral dies, its rocky, white skeleton remains. Over the course of many years, the limestone builds up to form coral reefs.

The Australian government's Department of the Environment and Heritage provides online information about the Great Barrier Reef and other World Heritage Areas in Australia.

EDITOR'S CHOICE

Access this Web site from http://www.myreportlinks.com

Early biologists mistook the colorful corals for plants. Actually they are animals related to jellyfish. Each coral polyp has a sac-like body with a single mouth hole. Like jellyfish, the polyps have stinging tentacles that help them catch their food. Corals use their skeletons for protection. During the day they remain hidden. At night they use their tentacles to catch food. Although coral polyps are carnivores, much of their energy comes from algae. The algae, called zooxanthellae, are microscopic plants. They grow inside the tissues of the coral.[2] It is the zooxanthellae that give the coral its color.

▷ Future in Peril

In 1975, Australia formed the Great Barrier Reef Marine Park. The reef is protected and closely managed by the Australian government. Tourists visit the park year-round. Scuba divers experience the underwater kingdom up close. The Great Barrier Reef has been around for ages. Even so, biologists worry that it is very fragile. Pollution is altering the earth's climate, and the Great Barrier Reef is not immune. The Australian Marine Park Authority has found evidence that the reefs are not growing as quickly as in the past. They blame this on pollution, which causes higher nitrogen levels in the water.[3] Warming ocean waters have also spelled trouble for the reefs over the last ten years. Coral is very sensitive to temperature changes. When the water is warmer than usual, the coral lose their zooxanthellae. This process is called coral bleaching because it often leaves the corals white. Coral can survive for only short periods without algae.[4]

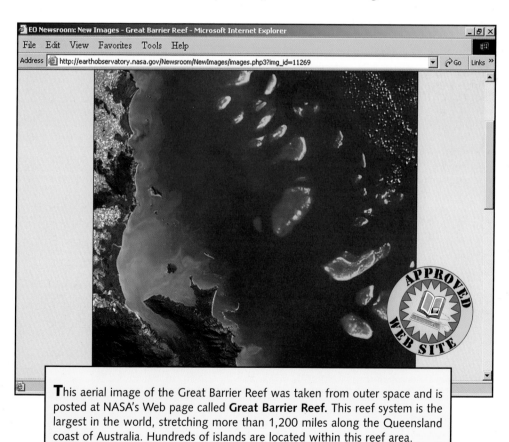

This aerial image of the Great Barrier Reef was taken from outer space and is posted at NASA's Web page called **Great Barrier Reef.** This reef system is the largest in the world, stretching more than 1,200 miles along the Queensland coast of Australia. Hundreds of islands are located within this reef area.

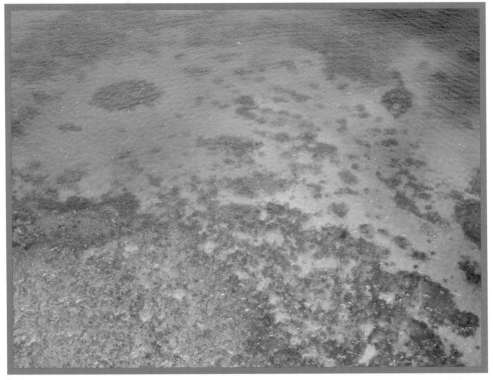

△ *A close-up look at the Great Barrier Reef from just above shallow water.*

Pollution is not the only threat to the reefs. A spine-covered starfish is another problem. The crown-of-thorns starfish is a predator that feeds on the coral. The starfish have lived in the Great Barrier Reef for thousands of years. However, in the 1960s, scientists first noticed an outbreak of starfishes. An "outbreak" means there are too many starfishes feeding on a coral colony. When this happens, the colony is badly damaged and may die. Scientists are unsure how quickly a colony will grow back, if at all. Within the last twenty-five years, there have been two serious outbreaks of starfishes.[5] Only time will tell how the Great Barrier Reef will handle these challenges.

Chapter 6 ▶

NORTHERN LIGHTS

Ribbons of green light stretch in an arc through the dark night sky. The glow shimmers and then fades. In another part of the heavens, a rose-colored flame intensifies. The color shifts, stretching and widening as you watch. Stars twinkle, visible through the curtains of color. The Northern Lights dance mysteriously in the night. They are high overhead, 60 miles (97 kilometers) above the earth's surface.[1] Suddenly the sky is dark again, leaving you to wonder if you imagined it all.

▲ The Northern Lights, or aurora borealis, are intense stretches of light. The shimmering glow of the lights is a breathtaking sight.

Unlike the other wonders of the world, the Northern Lights can only be seen at certain times and then only from high northerly latitudes. The lights also go by another name: *aurora borealis.* In Latin, *aurora* means the "red light of dawn." *Borealis* translates to "northerly." A mirror image of the Northern Lights is visible near the South Pole. The Southern Lights, or *aurora australis,* are simply not as famous as their northern cousins. Few people live far enough south to see them.

▷ Myths and Legends

There are many stories about the mysterious, shimmering glow in the north sky. Only in the last century have scientists been able to explain what the Northern Lights are. Before modern science, people struggled to make sense of the aurora. Often people were frightened of the lights. They thought the glowing red sky was a sign warning them about bad things to come.

The native people of Scandinavia, known as Laplanders, believed the Northern Lights were messengers of God. On nights when the lights streaked through the skies, Laplanders fell silent and looked toward the ground. They tried not to make any noise for fear they might make the lights angry. To show their respect, they looked away and went indoors. Vikings thought the lights were spears held by the Valkyries. The Valkyries were a sort of angel sent by Odin, the god of war, to decide who would die in battle.[2]

To the people of Finland, the lights looked like flames of a magical fire. They told legends of creatures called fire foxes. The foxes lit fire to the sky with sparks from their fur. The Finnish word for aurora translates as "fox fires." In North America, the Inuit people call the aurora *aqsalijaat,* which means "the trail of those who play soccer."[3] They believed the lights were spirits of the dead playing a soccer match.

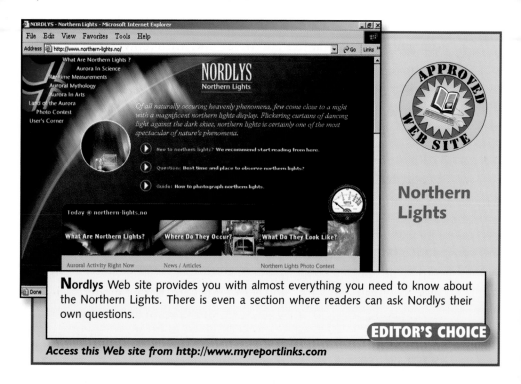

Nordlys Web site provides you with almost everything you need to know about the Northern Lights. There is even a section where readers can ask Nordlys their own questions.

Access this Web site from http://www.myreportlinks.com

▶ Birkeland Solves Mystery

A man named Kristian Birkeland was the one to solve the puzzle of the Northern Lights. Birkeland lived in Norway in the late 1800s. He was a physicist (a scientist who studies the forces of the physical world). Birkeland was interested in the invisible powers of electricity and magnets. It was well known that the *aurora borealis* occurred near the magnetic North Pole. Birkeland wondered why. How were the Northern Lights related to Earth's magnetic field? To find out, Birkeland spent a perilous winter in the far north of Norway, near the Arctic Circle. He and his team observed the phenomenon from a hut on a mountain peak. He brought instruments to record changes in the magnetic field.

Birkeland discovered that there were magnetic storms whenever the aurora glowed in the sky. He thought a powerful stream of energy must cause the magnetic storms. The only thing powerful enough was the Sun. He theorized that the Sun sent energy toward the Earth.

Solar Wind

Today we know that the Northern Lights are caused by bursts of energy from the Sun called the solar wind. The solar wind blasts toward Earth at the incredible speed of 500 miles (805 kilometers) a second. The forceful stream reaches Earth about three days later.[4] Fortunately, most of the stream never comes anywhere near our atmosphere. A magnetic shield around Earth repels it. This shield, called the magnetosphere, extends 40,000 miles (64,360 kilometers) out into space. Without the magnetosphere, the hot solar wind would scorch our planet.

When solar activity is high the sun releases solar particles. These particles travel with solar winds towards the Earth and are drawn into the atmosphere by the earth's magnetic field.

Many ancient people believed that auroras were an act of an angry god. In medieval times, people commonly attributed wars and disasters to the lights. Fantastic images such as this one are on display at the Web site called **Northern Lights** by Sigurdur H. Stefnisson.

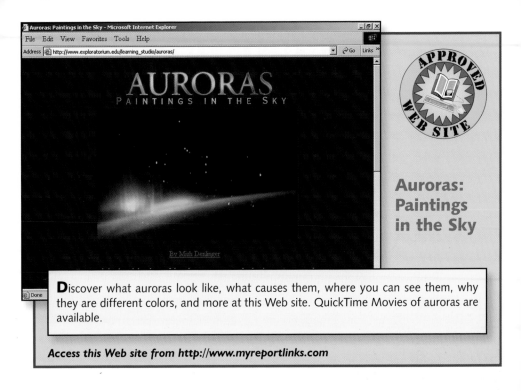

Access this Web site from http://www.myreportlinks.com

Very small bits of the solar wind escape through the shield. They enter the earth's atmosphere and are pulled down toward the magnetic poles. The earth's atmosphere is made up of gases. Oxygen and hydrogen are the most common. Particles from the solar wind bump into the gases. When these particles hit, they release energy. We see this energy in the form of light. Oxygen releases a green light. Hydrogen forms shades of pink, purple, and red.

Although Birkeland had discovered the answer, the scientific world did not believe him during his lifetime. In 1962, the American spacecraft *Mariner II* found evidence of the solar wind. Then people realized Birkeland's theories had been largely correct.[5] Solving the mystery did not make the auroras any less impressive, though. The flickering Northern Lights are still one of the most amazing sights of the natural world.

PARICUTÍN VOLCANO

Nothing is more terrifying than a volcanic eruption. Red-hot, molten rock escapes from deep inside the earth. Sometimes this lava trickles slowly from a hole in the ground. It may shoot up violently from a roaring volcano cone. Lava flows can cover the ground in a wave, destroying everything in their path. Volcano cones release clouds of hot ash and foul-smelling, toxic gases.

There are thousands of active volcanoes on our planet. Many erupt unseen on the ocean floor. Most volcanoes grow over the course of thousands of years. New volcanoes are extremely rare. So, in 1943, when a fledgling volcano rose up from the ground in Paricutín, Mexico, the world watched in shock and amazement.

▶ The Earth's Layers

Have you ever stopped to think about what is under the ground

◁ Imagine how frightening it would be to look out of the window and see a volcano erupting in the distance. That is exactly what happened to the residents of Paricutín, Mexico, on February 20, 1943.

we walk on? First there is the rock bed that forms earth's outer crust. In its deepest interior, the earth has a fiery hot metal core. There is a thick layer of rock between the crust and the core. This is the mantle. The mantle rock is so hot that it would be liquid were it not under intense pressure. While the pressure keeps most of the mantle solid, there are pockets of liquid metal called magma. When magma finds a crack in the earth's crust, it works its way to the surface, creating a volcano. Magma is called lava once it reaches the surface of the earth. Volcanoes and earthquakes happen most often where the tectonic plates meet. As the plates collide, the ground shakes and shifts—an earthquake has occurred.

▷ From Cornfield to Volcano

The Paricutín volcano is named after the town it destroyed. Paricutín is located in the Michoacan region of Mexico, about two hundred miles (three hundred kilometers) to the west of Mexico City. Ancient volcanoes formed the lush, rolling hills and fields of this part of Mexico. Long ago, the green hills had been volcano cones. Lava flows had covered the fields. Over time, the lava had broken down into rich soil.

Before the volcano was created in 1943, native Tarascan Indians and Spanish-speaking Mexicans had lived in Paricutín. Underneath their fertile farmland, the earth's crust was shifting. A Tarascan farmer named Dionisio Pulido owned the cornfield where the volcano began. In January 1943, he and other villagers noticed an increasing number of earthquakes. He grew used to feeling the ground rumble underneath his feet as he worked in his fields. Sometimes he would hear loud, thundering noises coming from underground, like huge boulders tumbling together. On February 20, 1943, after two weeks of strong earthquakes, Pulido saw a crack appear in the ground. He later recalled ". . . I felt a thunder, the trees trembled, and I turned to speak to [my wife]; and it was then I saw how, in the hole, the ground swelled and

▲ The Paricutín Volcano erupted for nine years, destroying the entire village that it was named for. However, scientists were able to learn a lot about volcanoes during this time.

raised itself two or two and a half meters [8 feet] high, and a kind of smoke, or fine dust—gray, like ashes—began to rise up."[1]

A smell of sulfur arose from the hole. Nearby plants and trees caught fire, lit by the fiery ash. More trench-like cracks grew in the ground. Within the first day, the cone grew to the size of a small hill, 98 feet (30 meters) in the air. On the second day, red-hot molten lava began to flow from cracks called vents. Frightened villagers fled from their homes. Thousands of people evacuated the area.

In a month, the volcano grew to 485 feet (148 meters). It rained down a thick layer of ash for 3 to 5 miles (5 to 8 kilometers) around. No people were injured, but the town of Paricutín was destroyed. First, volcanic ash covered the villagers' houses and fields. Then, the lava formed a slow-moving wall of rubble. The lava flow overtook the village over a year later.[2] In the nearby town of San Juan Parangaricutiro, only the church towers remained to rise above the lava. In 1952, the volcano grew quiet as quickly as it had begun. At its final height of 1,391 feet (424 meters), the mountain towered over nearby fields.

The volcano at Paricutín was a true wonder because a handful of people were there to see its birth. Scientists arrived as early as the second day. They were able to study firsthand how the volcano grew during the course of its nine-year lifetime. They gained valuable information about how volcanoes are created. Though the Paricutín volcano now lies dormant, its birth remains one of the Seven Wonders of the Natural World.

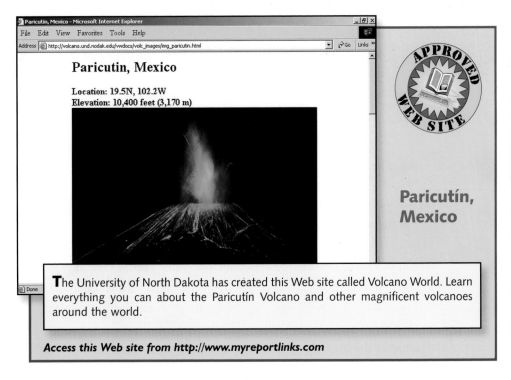

Paricutin, Mexico - Microsoft Internet Explorer

File   Edit   View   Favorites   Tools   Help

Address http://volcano.und.nodak.edu/vwdocs/volc_images/img_paricutin.html   Go   Links »

Paricutin, Mexico

Location: 19.5N, 102.2W
Elevation: 10,400 feet (3,170 m)

Paricutín, Mexico

The University of North Dakota has created this Web site called Volcano World. Learn everything you can about the Paricutín Volcano and other magnificent volcanoes around the world.

Access this Web site from http://www.myreportlinks.com

Back	Forward	Stop	Review	Home	Explore	Favorites	History

Chapter 8 ▶

HARBOR OF RIO DE JANEIRO

The Portuguese sailors under the direction of Captain André Goncalves and Gaspar de Lemos must have thought they had found paradise. While exploring the east coast of South America, they stumbled upon the most beautiful natural harbor on earth. The date was January 1, 1502. The sailors mistook the mile-wide harbor opening for the mouth of a great river. They misnamed the area, calling it *Rio de Janeiro,* the River of January. Tamoio

▲ The city of Rio de Janeiro, Brazil, with the harbor in the distance. Many consider this to be the most beautiful harbor in the world.

Indians lived near the harbor long before Europeans arrived. Knowing it better, they gave it the name Guanabara Bay. In the Tupi language, this means "arm of the sea."

Rio de Janeiro has one of the most well-protected harbors in the world. The entrance to Guanabara Bay is one mile (1.6 kilometers) wide. Once inside, the welcoming bay widens considerably. It is 18 miles (29 kilometers) long. However, what makes Rio one of the Seven Wonders of the Natural World is the awesome sight of it. There are mountains on all sides, stretching right down to the shore. Rocky hills extend out into the water. Nearly one hundred islands dot the bay. The curving, white-sand shoreline extends for miles. Climate plays an important role, too. Located just north of the Tropic of Capricorn, the weather is generally warm and pleasant year-round. The temperature averages between 76°F and 81°F (23°C and 27°C).[1]

A Place in the Sun

Pao de Acucar, an ancient rounded mound of rock, juts up out of the bay. In English, the name translates to "Sugar Loaf." The Portuguese settlers named it after the rounded loaves of sugar once made on the Portuguese island of Madeira. Tourist guidebooks highly recommend taking in the view from the top. A cable car runs up the mountain, but heartier sightseers hike one of the many trails to the summit. To the west of the harbor stands Mount Corcovado (Hunchback Mountain). On top of this hill is a remarkable 700-ton (635-metric-ton) sculpture of Christ the Redeemer. With its arms open wide, the hundred-foot statue seems to welcome people to this glorious spot.

The center of the city stands along Botafogo Bay, which opens into the much larger Guanabara Bay. The world-famous beaches of Ipanema and Copacabana are nearby. They are free for all to use. Often the beaches are jam-packed with people soaking up the sun. To the north of the city, the Organ Mountain range stretches off into the distance. Dense, green rain forests cover the hillsides.

The Marvelous City

Unlike the other wonders of the natural world, many people live amidst the splendor of Rio's harbor. In the 1890s, the shipping industry was at its peak. Rio's harbor made it one of the most important and largest cities in the world.[2] It was the capital of Brazil until the 1960s when the seat of government moved to Brasília. Rio continues to play an important role in the Brazilian economy and culture. At the start of the twenty-first century, it was Brazil's second-largest city. More than 5.5 million people called it home. Skyscrapers tower over the wide, sandy beaches.

Crammed between the mountains and the harbor, the city has little place left to grow. To make more room, the city planners flattened some hills. They used the soil to fill in parts of the harbor. Many people inhabit makeshift shantytowns on the

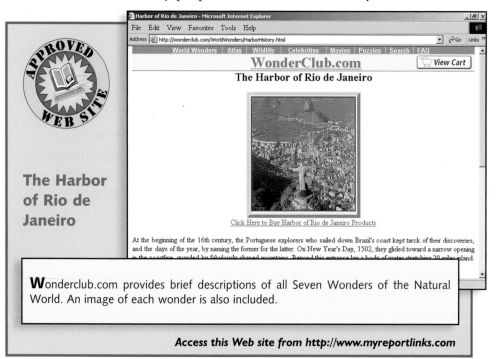

The Harbor of Rio de Janeiro

Wonderclub.com provides brief descriptions of all Seven Wonders of the Natural World. An image of each wonder is also included.

Access this Web site from http://www.myreportlinks.com

▲ Because it is so close to the city, the Harbor of Rio de Janeiro has experienced a good deal of pollution. Yet, efforts are being made to keep it among the world's most appealing waterways.

hillsides above the harbor. They live without running water or proper sanitation. City buildings and streets crowd right up to the waterfront. Pollution of the harbor is a significant problem. Still, the lush hillsides, city skyline, and sparkling water make the harbor area one of the most beautiful spots on earth.

Report Links

The Internet sites described below can be accessed at http://www.myreportlinks.com

▶ **The Seven Natural Wonders of the World**
Editor's Choice Learn about wonders of the natural world at this Web site.

▶ **Grand Canyon National Park**
Editor's Choice The National Park Service site about Grand Canyon National Park.

▶ **Great Barrier Reef Marine Park Authority**
Editor's Choice Learn about the issues that threaten the Great Barrier Reef.

▶ **Northern Lights**
Editor's Choice Aurora Borealis is nature's own fireworks.

▶ ***NOVA* Online: Everest**
Editor's Choice Learn about human exploration of Mount Everest.

▶ **Zambia National Tourist Board: The Victoria Falls**
Editor's Choice An online resource about the majestic Victoria Falls.

▶ **Aurora Borealis: Northern Lights**
This Web site describes the true cause of the aurora borealis.

▶ **Auroras: Paintings in the Sky**
QuickTime Movies of auroras are available at this location.

▶ **Everest 50**
Go on a virtual climb of Mount Everest.

▶ **EverestHistory.com: Time Line**
Read the history of Mount Everest's exploration.

▶ **Grand Canyon National Park: *National Geographic***
Take a virtual tour of the Grand Canyon.

▶ **Grand Canyon Slides**
View this collection of Grand Canyon photographs.

▶ **Great Barrier Reef**
Read more about the Great Barrier Reef at this NASA Web site.

▶ **Great Barrier Reef: *National Geographic***
A virtual dive in Australia's Great Barrier Reef.

▶ **The Great Barrier Reef**
Read about what makes this coral reef system special.

Any comments? Contact us: **comments@myreportlinks.com**

Report Links

▶ **The Harbor of Rio de Janeiro**
Learn why the wonder of Rio de Janeiro is its harbor.

▶ **How Are Coral Reefs Formed?**
This PBS Web site describes the formation of coral reefs.

▶ **Land Use History of Grand Canyon, Arizona**
Learn more about the history of the Grand Canyon.

▶ **Livingstone Discovers Victoria Falls, 1855**
Find out about David Livingstone's discovery of Victoria Falls.

▶ **Magnetic Storm: Gallery of Auroras**
View pictures of auroras taken with the Hubble Space Telescope.

▶ **Mosi-Oa-Tunya National Park**
Mosi-Oa-Tunya National Park is home to Victoria Falls.

▶ **Mount Everest History and Overview**
Get the facts about Mount Everest from this site.

▶ **Natural Wonders of the World: The Harbor of Rio de Janeiro**
This Web site provides a brief description of the Harbor of Rio de Janeiro.

▶ **Northern Lights by Sigurdur H. Stefnisson**
View images of the beautiful Northern Lights.

▶ **Paricutín**
You can read about the eruption of the Paricutín volcano.

▶ **Paricutín, Mexico**
A slide show and images of the volcano at Paricutín, Mexico.

▶ **Paricutín Volcano**
This Web site provides a brief description of the Paricutín volcano.

▶ **Rio de Janeiro**
Explore the history of Rio de Janeiro and its harbor.

▶ **Savage Earth: Out of the Inferno: Volcanoes**
This Web site from PBS describes volcanoes and their eruptions.

▶ **Victoria Falls: Zambezi River**
Study an aerial image of Victoria Falls.

aurora—A phenomenon in the upper atmosphere above a planet's magnetic polar regions where bands of light are created by the interaction between charged particles from the Sun and the planet's magnetic field.

continental shelf—A gradually deepening ocean floor from the edge of a continent to the deepest points of the ocean.

coral—A hard skeleton of a marine polyp.

crown-of-thorns starfish—An ocean predator that feeds on the top of coral reefs.

geology—The scientific study of the origin, history, and structure of the earth based upon information collected from its rocks.

glacier—A large and slow-moving mass of ice.

gorge—A deep, narrow canyon or part of a canyon; chasm.

hallucination—Visual perception of the presence of objects that are not real.

molten—Combined together and made into liquid by heat.

outbreak—As it pertains to the Great Barrier Reef, a situation where a multitude of starfishes is feeding on a coral colony, causing it to erode severely.

plate tectonics—A geological theory stating that the earth's crust and upper mantle are made of several plates that constantly move at a slow pace and that the interaction of these plates is the cause of most of earth's geologic activity, including earthquakes.

porous—Having or full of tiny holes that allow matter to pass through a membrane in an animal or plant.

solar wind—Constant flow of charged particles from the Sun into the solar system.

Chapter 2. Mount Everest

1. Audrey Salkeld, *Climbing Everest: Tales of Triumph and Tragedy on the World's Highest Mountain* (Washington, D.C.: National Geographic Society, 2003), p. 28.

2. T. R. Reid, "The Sherpas," *National Geographic,* May 2003, p. 56.

3. Michael Klesius, "The Body: Adjust or Die," *National Geographic,* May 2003, p. 33.

4. Liesl Clark with Broughton Coburn, "World of the Sherpa," *NOVA Online Expedition: Everest,* n.d., <http://www.pbs.org/wgbh/nova/everest/history/sherpasworld2.html> (February 16, 2004).

Chapter 3. Victoria Falls

1. Martin Dugard, *Into Africa* (New York: Doubleday, 2003), p. 16.

2. Livingstone Tourism Association of Livingstone, Zambia, "History and Culture," n.d., <http://www.destinationzambia.com/> (February 20, 2004).

3. Dr. David Livingstone, "The Victoria Falls: Livingstone's First Sighting," *Zambia National Tourist Board,* n.d., <http://www.zambiatourism.com/welcome.htm> (February 21, 2004).

4. Zambia National Tourist Board, "The Victoria Falls: Mosi-O-Tunya National Park," n.d., <http://www.zambiatourism.com/travel/places/victoria.htm> (February 21, 2004).

5. Livingstone Tourism Association of Livingstone, Zambia. "Activities," n.d., <http://www.destinationzambia.com/> (February 21, 2004).

Chapter 4. The Grand Canyon

1. Edward Dolnick, *Down the Great Unknown* (New York: HarperCollins Publishers, 2001), p. 225.

2. National Geographic Society, "Into the Canyon," n.d., <http://www.nationalgeographic.com/books/grandcanyon/insights/index.html> (February 6, 2004).

3. Stanley S. Beus and Michael Morales, eds., *Grand Canyon Geology* (New York: Oxford University Press, 1990), p. 1.

4. President Theodore Roosevelt, "Address at Grand Canyon, AZ, May 6, 1903," from Ann and Myron Sutton, *The Wilderness World of the Grand Canyon: "Leave It As It Is"* (Philadelphia: J.B. Lippincott Company, 1971), p. 218.

Chapter 5. Great Barrier Reef

1. Great Barrier Reef Marine Park Authority, "GBR Explorer: Marine Invertebrates," n.d., <http://www.reefed.edu.au/explorer/animals/marine_invertebrates/index.html> (January 30, 2004).

2. Douglas H. Chadwick, "Kingdom of Coral: Great Barrier Reef," *National Geographic,* January 2001, p. 42.

3. Ibid., p. 52.

4. Great Barrier Marine Park Authority, "Coral Bleaching and Mass Bleaching Events," 2002, <http://www.gbrmpa.gov.au/corp_site/info _services/science/bleaching/index.html> (January 31, 2004).

5. Dr. Peter Moran, "Crown-of-Thorns Starfish Questions and Answers," Australian Institute of Marine Science On-Line Reference Series, 1997, <http://www.aims.gov.au/pages/reflib/cot-starfish/pages/cot-q34.html> (January 31, 2004).

Chapter 6. Northern Lights

1. Mish Denlinger, "Auroras: Paintings in the Sky," n.d., <http:// www.exploratorium.edu/learning_studio/auroras/fromspace.html> (January 24, 2004).

2. Lucy Jago, *The Northern Lights* (New York: Alfred A. Knopf, 2001), p. 9.

3. Swedish Institute of Space Physics, "Northern Lights: Beliefs in Ancient Times," n.d., <http://www.irf.se/norrsken/Norrsken_history.html> (January 24, 2004).

4. Jago, p. 54.

5. Ibid., p. 272.

Chapter 7. Paricutín Volcano

1. James F. Luhr and Tom Simkin, eds., *Paricutín: The Volcano Born in a Mexican Cornfield* (Phoenix: Geoscience Press, Inc., 1993), p. 5.

2. Mary Nolan and Sid Nolan, "Human Communities and Their Responses," from James F. Luhr and Tom Simkin, eds., *Paricutín: The Volcano Born in a Mexican Cornfield* (Phoenix: Geoscience Press, Inc., 1993), p. 206.

Chapter 8. Harbor of Rio de Janeiro

1. Tourism Office of the Brazilian Embassy, "Visit Brazil: Climate," n.d., <http://www.braziltourism.org/faq4.shtml> (January 19, 2004).

2. Sergio Koreisha, "Rio de Janeiro, Brazil," n.d., <http://darkwing .uoregon.edu/~sergiok/brasil/rio.html> (January 17, 2004).

Bramwell, Martyn. *Africa.* Minneapolis, Minn.: Lerner, 2000.

Cox, Reg. *Seven Wonders of the Natural World.* Broomall, Pa.: Chelsea House Publications, 2000.

Gray, Shirley W. *Mexico.* Minneapolis, Minn.: Compass Point Books, 2001.

Gutnik, Martin, and Natalie Browne-Gutnik. *Great Barrier Reef.* Austin, Tex.: Steck-Vaughn, 1994.

Kent, Deborah. *Rio de Janeiro.* New York: Scholastic Library Publishing, 1996.

Luhr, James F. and Tom Simkin. *Paricutín: The Volcano Born in a Cornfield.* Tucson, Ariz.: Geoscience Press, Inc., 1993.

National Geographic Society Staff. *Experiences in the Grand Canyon.* Broomall, Pa.: Chelsea House Publishers, 1999.

Salkeld, Audrey. *Climbing Everest: Tales of Triumph and Tragedy on the World's Highest Mountain.* Washington, D.C.: National Geographic Society, 2003.

Stevens, Rebecca. *Everest.* New York: DK Publishing, 2001.

Van Rose, Susanna. *Eyewitness: Volcano and Earthquake.* New York: DK Publishing, 2000.

Worth, Richard. *Stanley and Livingstone and the Exploration of Africa in World History.* Berkeley Heights, N.J.: Enslow Publishers, Inc., 2000.